W9-BQU-629

BUILD A BRAIN

By Kirsty Holmes

HOW TO BUILD A HUMAN BODY

Enslow PUBLISHING

Published in 2021 by Enslow Publishing, LLC
101 W. 23rd Street, Suite 240,
New York, NY 10011

Copyright © 2021 Booklife Publishing
This edition is published by arrangement with Booklife Publishing

Cataloging-in-Publication Data

Names: Holmes, Kirsty.
Title: Build a brain / Kirsty Holmes.
Description: New York : Enslow Publishing, 2021. | Series: How to
build a human body | Includes glossary and index.
Identifiers: ISBN 9781978519152 (pbk.) | ISBN 9781978519176
(library bound) | ISBN 9781978519169 (6 pack)
Subjects: LCSH: Brain--Juvenile literature. | Nervous system--
Juvenile literature.
Classification: LCC QP376.H65 2020 | DDC 612.8'2--dc23

Printed in the United States of America

CPSIA compliance information: Batch #BS20ENS: For further information
contact Enslow Publishing, New York, New York at 1-800-542-2595

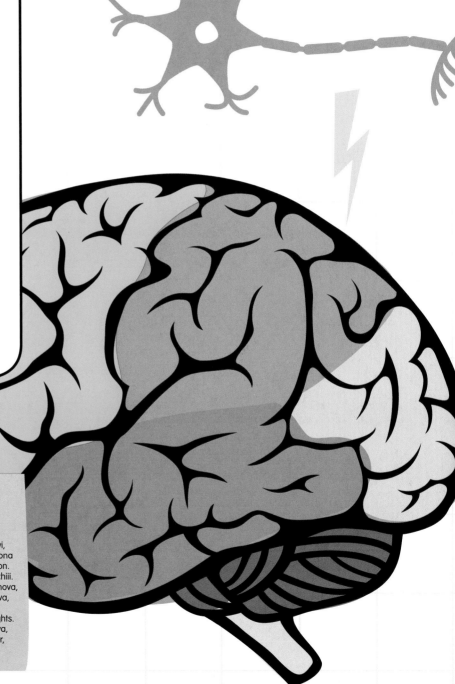

Photo credits:

**Images are courtesy of Shutterstock.com.
With thanks to Getty Images, Thinkstock Photo
and iStockphoto.**

Ian Struction – gjee. Grid – DistanceO. Front Cover – maglyvi,
GzP_Design. 4 –VitalasArts. 5 – Andy Frith. 6–7 – eveleen, Aliona
SmartArt, Lorelyn Medina, Pro Symbols, Anatolir, WhiteDragon.
8 – EgudinKa. 10 –VitalasArts. 11 – GzP_Design. 12–13 – Achiichii.
14 – MIKHAIL GRACHIKOV. 15 – Dragana Eric. 18 – Farah Sadikhova,
Anatolir, T–Kot, Tomas Knopp, Nadiinko, Tarana Mammadova,
kosmofish, RaulAlmu. 19 – Line – design, Melin Creative.
20–21 – bioraven, quka, Irina Sulima, Pranch, AVIcon, Polar_lights.
22– iconim, Farah Sadikhova, Webicon, Tarana Mammadova,
Drk_Smith, AVIcon, Andi Muhammad Hasbi H, GoperVector,
ductru, NeMaria, Vector Market, Fox Design, kosmofish.
23 – LUCKY_CAT, Katrina Lee.

CONTENTS

Words that look like <u>this</u> can be found in the glossary on page 24.

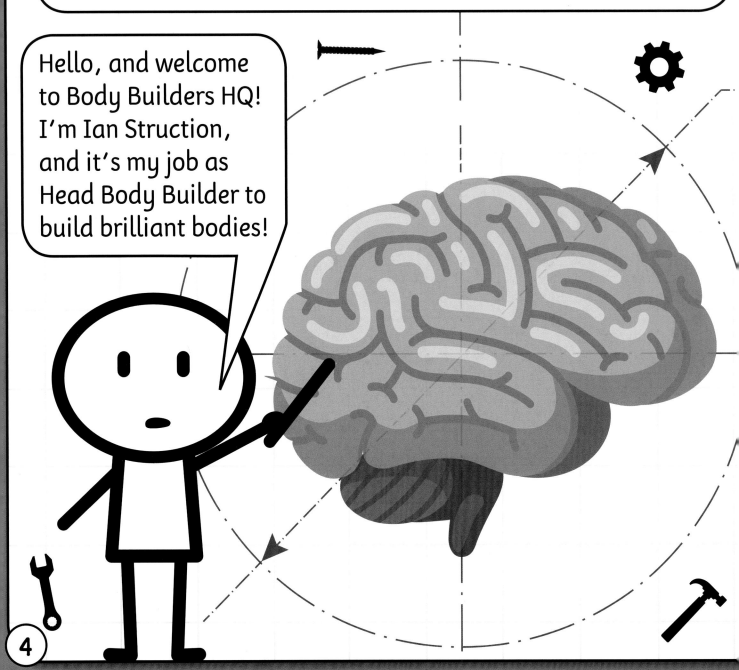

This instruction manual will teach you all about the human brain. Look out for these signs to help you understand:

Do this

Don't do this

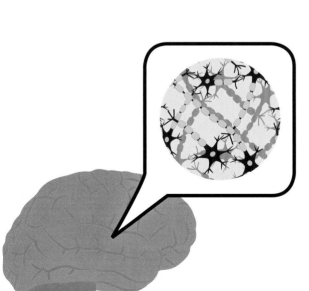

Zoom in on details

More information

THE HUMAN BODY

There are lots of parts that work together in the human body. We build each body full of amazing <u>organs</u>, which all have special jobs to do.

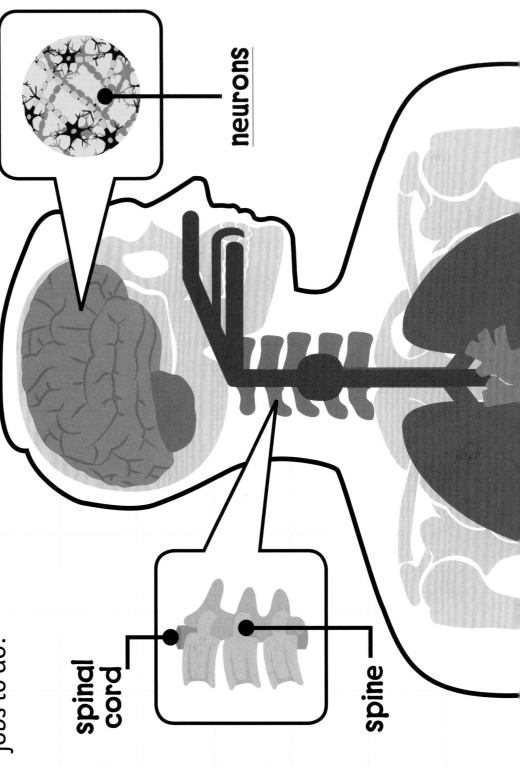

neurons

spinal cord

spine

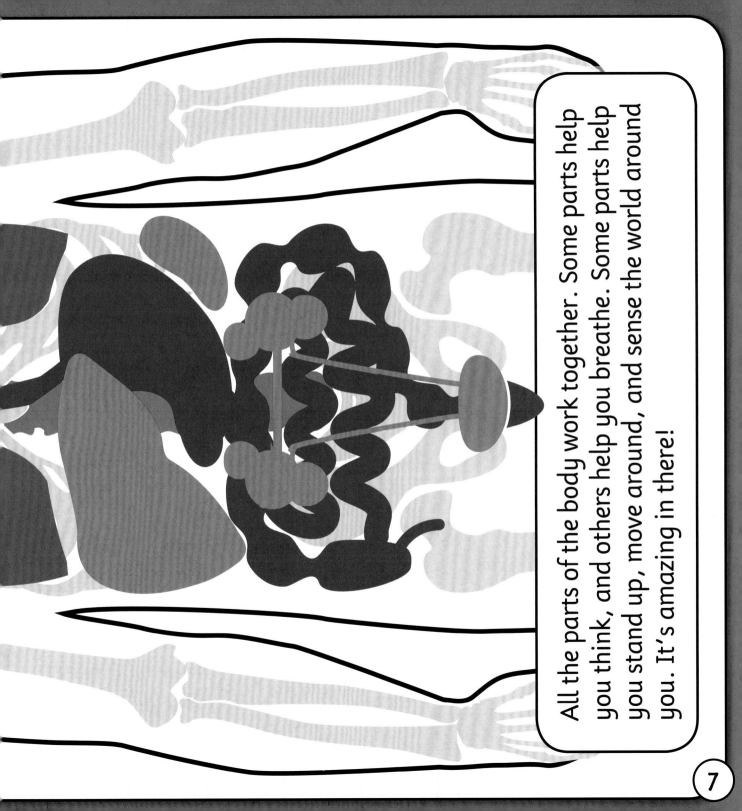

All the parts of the body work together. Some parts help you think, and others help you breathe. Some parts help you stand up, move around, and sense the world around you. It's amazing in there!

THE HUMAN BRAIN

The human brain is a complicated and very important organ. It acts as a kind of supercomputer for the body, taking in information and telling the other body parts and <u>systems</u> what to do.

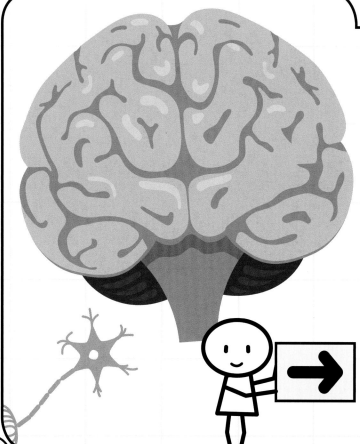

- like a computer for the body

- takes in information

- makes decisions

- runs all the other systems

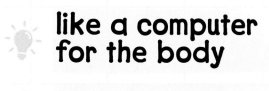

New brain <u>cells</u> are being made all the time, even in older people.

Around three-quarters of your brain is made up of water. If you don't drink enough water, you could get a headache and find it difficult to think clearly.

The cerebrum is the biggest part of your brain. Most thinking happens here.

The cerebellum controls balance and <u>coordination</u>.

The brain stem controls things you do without thinking about them, such as breathing and swallowing.

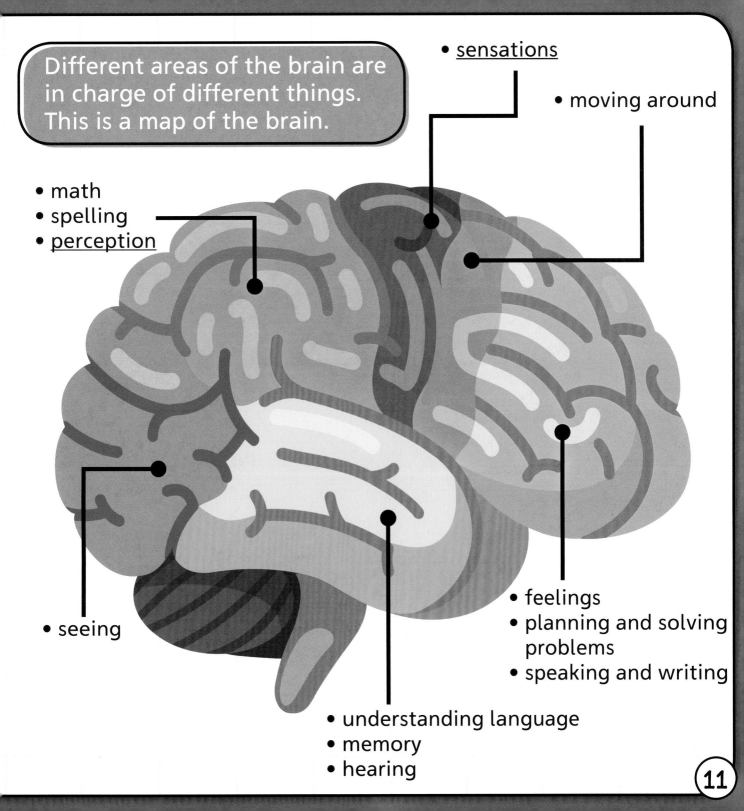

Different areas of the brain are in charge of different things. This is a map of the brain.

- sensations
- moving around
- math
- spelling
- perception
- seeing
- feelings
- planning and solving problems
- speaking and writing
- understanding language
- memory
- hearing

The brain might be the cleverest organ, but it can't do much without the rest of the body! For the brain to work properly, we will also need:

Nerves
Nerves are tiny bundles of <u>fibers</u> that carry information.

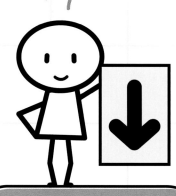

Motor neurons carry information from the brain to the <u>muscles</u>, telling them what to do.

The human body has around 100 billion nerves.

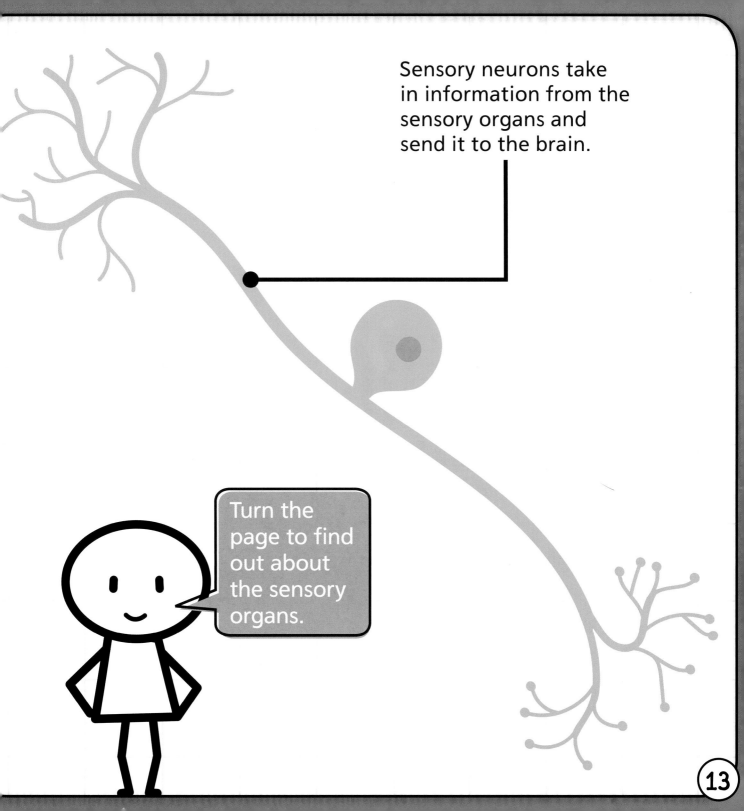

Sensory neurons take in information from the sensory organs and send it to the brain.

Turn the page to find out about the sensory organs.

The Sensory Organs

The sensory organs are the organs that take in information from the world around you. They are:

1x nose

smell

1x skin

touch and temperature

2x **eyes**

sight

2x ears

hearing

1x tongue

taste

1x **spinal cord**

This is the main pathway where all the messages from around the body travel to get to the brain. The spinal cord is made up of nerves and runs down the middle of the back. It is protected by bones.

nerves from the spinal cord

bones of the spine

The skin is the largest organ in the body.

CARE FOR YOUR BRAIN: EXERCISE

Physical exercise is not just good for the body. It is also really good for the brain! Exercise makes your heart beat faster, and this sends more <u>oxygen</u> to the brain, helping it work better.

Why not try:

running

push-ups

sit-ups

swimming

cycling

basketball

tennis

weights

Any exercise that gets your heart pumping is also good for your brain.

dancing

jumping

skipping rope

trampoline

ball games

kickboxing

CARE FOR YOUR BRAIN: FOOD

You can eat some of these brain-boosting foods every day!

green leafy vegetables

red peppers

carrots

nuts

berries

whole grain bread

seafood

chicken and turkey

Some foods that taste good don't support brain health.

sugary drinks

fast food

salt

pastries

candy

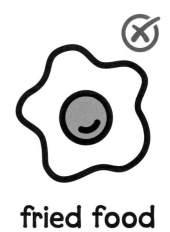

fried food

CARE FOR YOUR BRAIN: BRAIN TRAINING

Memory games, puzzles, and thinking problems can all help you learn, grow and stretch your brain, and improve your memory.

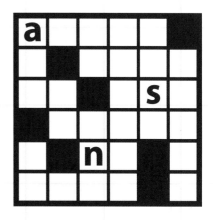

crosswords

jigsaw puzzles

video games

building with bricks

guessing games

memory games

spot the difference

Time to train that brain!

Memory Madness!

Look at all the pictures on this page for one minute. Then close the book and see how many you can remember. No cheating!

A-MAZE-ing!

Can you follow the maze with your finger to help the nerve send a signal to the brain?

GLOSSARY

cells the basic units that make up all living things

coordination when the body's muscles work together

fibers things that are like threads

muscles parts of the body that can squeeze together to make something move

neurons single nerve cells

organs parts of a living thing that have specific, important jobs to do to keep the body working properly

oxygen a natural gas that living things need in order to survive

perception understanding the world by using your senses

sensations information sent from the sensory organs to the brain

systems sets of things that work together to do specific jobs

INDEX